I0202504

Deep Territory

Deep Territory

poems by

Michael Malan

BLUE LIGHT PRESS ◆ 1ST WORLD PUBLISHING

1st WORLD
PUBLISHING

SAN FRANCISCO ◆ FAIRFIELD ◆ DELHI

DEEP TERRITORY
Copyright ©2021 by Michael Malan

All rights reserved. Printed in the United States of America. No part of this book may be used or reproduced in any manner whatsoever without written permission except in the cases of brief quotations embodied in critical articles and reviews. For information contact:

1ST WORLD LIBRARY
PO Box 2211
Fairfield, IA 52556
www.1stworldpublishing.com

BLUE LIGHT PRESS
www.bluelightpress.com
Email: bluelightpress@aol.com

COVER ART
Deanna Tubb-Sedillo

AUTHOR PHOTOGRAPH
Roberta Sperling

FIRST EDITION

Library of Congress Catalog-in-Publication Data

ISBN 9781421837031

for my brothers and sisters in Spirit

CONTENTS

III. A SMALL TREE IN A GLASS BOWL

I

A Bell Ringing in a Broken Tower

The Night Air

I want to write about the forest
that is like a city and a city
that is like a playground
where my eyes are locked doors
and the keys to the forest
are hung in the cemetery
where the children of Love
are singing the ancient hymns,
and darkness is reflected
in stainless-steel towers
beside a river where the wealthy
are kissing their lucky mirrors
and the stars of creation
are ambling across the night sky
like they've got no place to go.
I will lie down in that place
that no longer exists
and feel the night air tickling my toes.

My Grandmother's House

A man holding a lantern
passes me on the trail above
the waterfall where my grandmother
camped for years before
the Spirit called her.
She walked slowly to the river,
cast her silence into the air.
Her words have been forgotten,
but not her stories and dreams,
which will remain forever.
I cannot find the stream behind
her house, the souls of trees,
or the *cenoté* where they originated.
I learned little there except
how to chant the old songs
and beat the drums of my ancestors.
When I open a window,
the summer breeze is like
a candle burning in a barn,
her long skirt a tent for the living.

We Were Not Born to Forget

In the stillness of perfection,
the room where I sleep
is dark like the resistance
we feel when our hearts are cold.
What we forgot in the shadow
of the river, patience and serenity,
I am trying to remember.
I kneel in a sacred place
and dream of my brothers
and sisters who are asleep
in the bosom of a different legend.
They step away from the forest
and place their hands
on the body of the world.
True being is the life we lead
when we approach
the pure light of adoration.

Stargazer

Life is like sleep, the sound of windows
closing and doors opening,
a voice from the closet, friends
who speak to you from another country
where shadows are singing
or sleeping under great flowering trees.
Clouds bring rain and the man
painting your fence smiles as night
saunters down from the mountains.
When the last star has fallen,
the woodcutter will rise from his bed
and the trees will shiver in their winter clothes.
Stargazer, how many have slept
in the windows of your eyes?
In this country, roads flow like rivers
at the memory of your touch.
I will ask you to stay just one night
and fly with me through dreams of heaven.

A Song of the Forest

I do not wonder about immortality.
I spend my days stringing
and unstringing my bow.
This window that looks out on a field
of wheat is a door to another world.
Streets run between clouds.
Dogs run between streets.
In each house, silence is a touchstone
in the divine economy.

A bird flew down my chimney
and perched on my arm,
offered me a gift, a song of the forest,
a hymn of the meadow.
My ancestors are calling from the place
where dreams are revealed.
When I leave here I will follow the path
that leads to the country where
a primeval forest is breaking
like a wave on rainbow waters.

In the Country Where I Was Born

When we were children we ran in the glen,
picked wildflowers and decorated
our hair with spidery webs. We gathered
dew into buckets and hung the mirrors
of the forest on the tree of innocence.
Our eyes were like cloisters, like torn calendars
on the walls of one-room schoolhouses.

Everything exists in the mind, in memory,
in rocks washed away in a flood.
Running in slow motion between rivers
of starlight, every wound healed quickly,
lovingly, like a flowering plant in the wilderness.
There is no death or dying here.
Just as our fathers and mothers imagined,
leaves carry laughter in the wind.

Down to the sea, past ruined temples,
crossing a river in a jungle, finding a tomb
buried in eucalyptus trees. In the country
where I was born, men are praying
and praising God. We were not born to die,
but to live as waterfalls in the heaven
of our ancestors, to walk as spirits
in the forest of everything that is real.

My Brother Running

I hear voices in the mountains.
Wildflowers speaking softly, summer
remembering winter, the moon
hiding in a forest. Someone running,
not my brother, not the moon
swimming in a frozen lake,
not the lake breathing in the sun.
I have seen a white horse in the river.
I have seen lightning in the horse's tail.

In the next valley, horses are galloping
across a shallow river, across the meadow
where winter moths are born,
blind eyes in their wings opening.
Everything we have loved is here,
in the valley where trees are watching,
where the river carries the highway
beyond the mountains.

Coals in the campfire are like red faces,
voices in the stream like blue fire.
When night comes,
trees vanish and rivers sleep.
Each moment is a place we've been before,
a city born of its own voyage,
a village rising into being.
The openness of trees, the secrecy of mountains.
My brother running along this path, forever.

After Midnight, in the Presence of Angels

We were hungry for something else.
A riddle or unkind remark,
a suggestion that could get you into trouble.
A feeling that vanishes after a while
or hangs on forever. Frozen fog,
freedom from death, a ghost striding
streamlike into the mountains.
The mind within and without.
The trail ends here, in the valley
where the sky is like a blue workshirt.

Is time shifting now or making
a last stand in the power of language?
We are free to follow, free to enlarge the tent.
Move out into the brisk,
start home in subzero conditions.
When the shadow freezes,
the body dozes. Let's stay
stiff-muscled as the wolves approach.
This kind comes not with prayer and fasting,
but with a closer look at a kindling fire.

Everything I Do Involves Forgetting

At the river's source, beggars
are learning about the harmony
and beauty of the new economy.
They will embrace absence,
then clap their hands like a mirror
at the edge of the universe
where time waits for everyone.
I am wearing the horizon like a belt,
like a robe. A raven tells me
the path I am walking is closed.
At the top of the mountain
the old songs are forgotten.
When I think about this nation
of small towns and hamlets,
border villages, woodland cities,
and the farm where I learned
to speak the language of desire,
hills and valleys throw back
their heads, and the shadows
of bees are trampled underfoot.

These Words I Write

After we left the church, my brother
looked at me and smiled,
and suddenly I understood the river
as it washes away the guilt,
and the rain that heals the wounds
of lonely ranchers who draw
pictures of calves roping men.
Today I feel a great distance
between us and not the closeness
I felt among the castle rocks.
A light follows me from room
to room and when I go outside
and watch the winter moon blinking
and the stars growing larger
and the animal nature of things
watching, I slip back
into the joy of not being there.
These words I write will never take me home.

Where the Rivers Meet

Everything vanishing: time, illness, memory,
the body that rises and falls in the water,
the voice that raises its hand
when the river speaks.
Born of sun and moon,
dreaming of hummingbirds
and wildflowers, whispers
of wisdom from the Milky Way.
In the valley where rivers meet,
I will find everything I have lost.
I will embrace the people
who have traveled there before me.
In the future no more departures,
only arrivals and discoveries.
I will read books that have not been written
and fan the flame of a summer solstice.

The Road South

Cold water from the mountains,
hot stones from the sun.
Brother, I will take your picture
in the mountains where clouds
are blooming and the darkness
of the forest envelopes you.

You will always be there, in the wind,
in the rain, in the breeze through
the white curtains in your bedroom.
The body at rest, sleeping
in the language of reconciliation,
moon and mountains shaking hands.

I will fish the rivers of sorrow
and hunt the forests where
the wild men live forever.
Brother, I do not ask why you
travel north when the road south
is the more dangerous path.
Follow me as I follow the wind.

The First Day

My neighbor wanted to sell me punky
firewood, not cherry or ash,
but poverty and humility.
I have enough of these.
Words are like mirrors
and winter is a wet, green field,
harmony and light, fruit in a bowl,
not any bowl, but more
like a lonely path beside the sea,
or a long conversation
at the heart of an empty river.
Now he stands in front of my fireplace,
as the room grows smaller
and my dog tries to bark.
I feel not awe, but gratitude
for each lost moment
on the first day of his reappearing.

A Forgotten Language

I remember sitting beside a waterfall
and watching as a white church
appeared in the forest where torn flags sleep.
I wore a dark coat to the party,
left after the last dance, before the first prayer.
I am writing and thinking in a language
that was forgotten long ago,
when the first camels
climbed from a crater on the moon
and the clocks in the river
grew numb at the feet of broken glass.
The forest speaks to me of heavenly days,
of silver fish flooding a net of blue whales.
All pain vanishing as trees
lay hands on the rivers of tomorrow.

The Dogs of Winter

Far below, in the silence of dreams,
I could feel the harbor, dusk spreading,
fires burning in iron pots, planets
suddenly dark with the breath of clouds.
We are rest stops, not destinations.
We are grass where animals are grazing.
I will speak to my horse in the pasture
where the roots of trees are singing.

After twenty years, I have not found
the gate that leads to the city where life
is humming. Sea birds are flying west
toward the nature preserve, an island
off the coast where drowned sailors
fall in love with the blue sun
of endless journeys. In the mountains,
the dogs of winter are always barking.
I will play my flute and feed my fire.
I was not born to tread water.

Men from the East

Wherever I look there are islands
of flowers, metal creatures
bucking a silver highway,
a red ocean at the root of fire.
Birds, flowers, vistas of sunsets,
and fabulous cloud formations:
the Godhead revisited.
In the land of snow for a long time
breath melts, Scorpio slips down
around us like a pillow.
Valleys fill with rain and mountains
march toward the sea.
Men from the east say the earth
might quake, when shadows
speak and mirrors break.
Brother, sister, whatever you are to me,
take the rain by the hand, let it go.

My Father's House

We knelt in a circle and howled like wolves.
What we saw was like loneliness,
like the breath of an animal
climbing a mountain in our dreams.
There is only silence in the eye of the leaf
and in the tongue of the wind.
Each moment in the forest is like a lantern
in the clouds. When I pass by
I see wolves sleeping in a pool of stone.
I am riding a river into a village of light.
Bells are ringing, the ceremony is about to begin.
A spirit moves in the chapel,
a spirit moves in the glen.
At night we see my father's house, lit from within.

The Man at the Gate

Now is a time of natural
emotional awakening—
breath returning to life,
the sky as it becomes larger
and darker, a valley of peaks
and shadows, trees speaking
to one another quietly,
whispering in the darkness.
I feel spring in the wind
and summer in the rain.
Like a traveler lost in a forest
after years have passed
and his relatives suddenly
reappear: the man at the gate
wears his hat like a cloud.

The Sound of Darkness

I imagine that desire comes and goes
like the body that reaches
beyond the trees,
beyond the horizon,
where the planets are reeling,
stars catching fire.
Where I am living now
is like a clock ticking
in the house of forever,
a harness in the barn
where my white horse is waiting.
I am not afraid of the forest
where the flames
of death are burning.
I hear the sound of darkness
as it dances from lake to lake.
My spirit will not let me die.

The Path Beside the Stream

I am free now to feed the birds
singing in the square
surrounding the fountain
where dead slaves sleep
and free men and women recite verse
but have no faith in words:
their language is a god to the senses.
I am entering another country
with my eyes closed.
When I follow tracks beside a stream
I find bridges like locked doors
and planets buried in snow.
To cross now would mean
venturing inside
the lost shadow of the river.

Three Great Conversions

A lyric lying beside the road,
hit by a car, radiator ruined,
the lyric like an epoch one traverses
as one fails to apprehend
the three great conversions:
heart stuck with pins and needles,
head in a nest of hair,
purse that opens and closes
as men in black
file past women in blue,
who are traveling
in their own sweet, lyrical orbits.

In the twenty-fifth canto
fog lifts, lyric branches,
bifurcates, head and heart
temporarily in synch,
but not the purse.
The poet walks through the forest
on fire with the names
of centuries cast by the wayside,
sky on edge as she travels
from one country to the next,
during a time of peace
on the great ship of uncertainty.

Vision of the Past

On the wall is a postcard of a room
where I slept as a child
on a narrow wicker bed
with a blue coverlet.
Through the window I saw
a raised trestle and a steep canyon
where a narrow highway
looped back and forth
like a ribbon of light.

The underside of the taro leaf
is like a clock
that will not stop ticking.
In the center of the city
someone is afraid
or pretending to be a stone
in a bandaged hand.
I did not stop believing,
even when my vision of the past
jumped the river bank
and climbed the first wall of eternity.

My Friends in the Village

It is May and already the ocean is calling,
the wind clapping its hands.
This time last year I was standing
on a mountain looking over a wall
at a crescent moon,
and beyond that, Jupiter and Mars.
I remembered a poem
I had written years ago
and thought I had forgotten.

The trees understand what birds know
and what animals remember:
the land before time
when only trees lived here
and stars drifted beyond the shadows
that swim in the river
where the sun sinks like a flower
in the deepest pool.
My friends in the village
have neglected the mysterious
centers of thought.

II
Time Expands in a Universe of Silence

So Many Windows, So Many Passing Moments

In the mountains, between the stars,
when the sky is dreaming,
you feel free. A wave stirs in the pit
where the stones of forgetfulness
are healed. Screams are swallowed
in the cemetery where the hands
of clocks have replaced the sleeping city,
the locked door, the cautious glance.

At first light, trees sway and the ocean
dances in the sound of its own breath.
Doors open and a river too deep to cross
appears in the valley where clouds
blanket a sea of storms.
A woman on the beach tells me
there is a spirit rising in the waves,
like rain, like wind,
not the passing of hours,
but a prayer escaping from another world.

The Wolf of Summer

I try to remember that afternoon lying
on a blanket beside a lake,
the sun as dim as the eye of heaven,
the lake a breath in a giant's throat,
the blanket a carpet on the floor of eternity.
When I return to that place
I will tell my stories. I will talk about
Venus and Mars and people without hope
in a year of dread silence.
Elms and poplars are like brothers,
hophornbeam my closest friend.
My canoe is a bridge to distant rivers,
everything I will ever know
like an echo from the mountains.
The wolf of summer is running in the forest.

Crown of Remorse

Words take on different meanings
here in the desert.
Clouds speak for themselves,
the sky voluptuous,
planets like bowling balls.
My breath, after running a long distance,
the highway where it faltered
beside a wall of kisses.
The moon broken like a coffee cup—
I will show its picture
to the woman who left me
with the crown of remorse.
Let me tell you about the hounds
that are like islands,
like constellations
in another invisible winter.
It was so dark I could see stars in her hair.

When One Flower Blossoms

Spirit of sun and clouds, red vetch
and yellow clover, the banks
of the river exploding with bruises,
purple sage and timothy,
the underlying truth that sets
thought flying: star of revelation,
kiss of the water-rutted road.

Shadow of winter, bright promise
of luminosity, eyes suddenly
open to the idyllic nature of being:
we are all kin to ancient souls,
prophets of cedar, progenitors of light.
Revive us with your fire.

Salt of earth, thunder in the Soul
of souls, moments when emptiness
is blessed, a lantern lighting
an ocean of sky. A psalm never
spoken, only remembered,
a message of simplicity in a dream
of wakened sleep. Shadow of smoke,
union of wind and rain, song
of transfiguration: when one
flower blossoms, all flowers blossom.

What I Took with Me

I lived in all the big cities,
then I moved to a small town,
and then I moved again,
to the kingdom of everything
I desire, always on the go,
always alone with nothing
in the wind, nothing in the trees.
I left my coat on a bench,
my books on a bus.

Now I hear friends complain
about the weather or ask
to borrow my books.
I am like a dead teacher,
I tell them, find a another mentor,
a poet or novelist who lives
in darkness, wears feathers,
and beats a drum like a book.

Water flows through my arms
and into the sea. Mountains
fly away and take the snow
and clouds with them. The earth
is moving past the cottage
where the truth-teller lives.
She is not home today.
She is sitting in the snow,
breathing clouds like a horse.
Death does not speak to her anymore.
Her new country is in language.

Forsooth

At night, under the covers
with a flashlight, I lie in bed
reading *The Three Musketeers*.
I hear my parents in the hallway,
winter closing in around our house.
Next door, our neighbors
are watching TV, a drama
of life in the forest, a story
about frontier men in the mountains,
a series they watch every night
as the trees dance outside.

Downtown, a woman wearing
a skin-tight dress walks past
darkened windows,
hungry for the hand that touches
the air like summer,
like the song I heard as I was
walking in the rain,
past the cemetery where the souls
of pioneers and adventurers
are flying like pages in the wind.

Regeneration

Like a forgotten truth, far from home,
the silence reminds us that dawn
is far-flung, not the trees we remember
or the city that slipped through
our fingers, the love we sacrificed
on the altar of temptation.
Like a continent on the moon,
a sun drifting in a river of stars,
a traveler on a dusty road,
a language I have forgotten,
like weeks that sail past my window.
They are building a road
through my neighbor's orchard.
I do not remember when they first came
or when they left and took
the mountains with them.
On the hill behind my house
the windows of the hospital are open
and the patients' prayers drift overhead.

The River Beyond the Forest

At night, spirits move through
the rooms of my house,
through the windows of my mind,
and whisper psalms I will never forget.
When my father died, I slipped
off my shoes and walked barefoot
across the cemetery where he is buried
and all the other cemeteries
that were buried with him.

I am a different person now
that I have found the bridge
where who I was before drifted
into another realm. I hear
my father's footsteps in the songs
the saints sing as they march
through forests that one day
will become monuments
in the land of forgiveness.

When I open the door
that leads to the river that flows
to the graves of my ancestors,
I hear their voices calling to the trees
that will never stop listening.
I wonder if the river will be there
when I am ready to sail away.

Dream City

I look through windows as I walk
and the windows look back at me
and smile. The doors are open
and cheerful. I hear singing
in the larger houses and poetry
recited in bungalows. I run
and am not weary—sidewalks
comfort me. An entire day
given to laughter. Daydream
after daydream, I hear a storm
crawling across the plains.
I count my blessings as night
sneaks into my life through
a back alley. Silence everywhere
is like a story I could not stop
reading. Tonight, as I sleep,
I am living in an unfamiliar city
and cannot find my way home.

Years That Never End

Almost everything is a source of revelation:
sunlight on the mountains,
a plant emerging from the soil.
Trees are different somehow, more alive—
they want to tell you their stories.
You feel relaxed, comfortable
with your forest friends.
Everything they say is clearly understood.
Some will be seekers, others
revolutionaries. One is tending
a garden of white roses,
another hunting jaguars in the jungle.
Wild years, immature years,
years that fade away, years that never end.

Tomorrow Is Not Just Another Day

I was born in the forest,
but get bored easily, so I moved
to the forest within the forest
and rented a room in the tallest tree.
Every leaf in my forest
is an ancestral figure,
an invisible face, a stone icon
projected on a wall of grief,
a wave breaking on a beach
cluttered with ancient civilizations.
Each ornament on my special tree
is a distant planet: blue, green,
gold, red, spinning in space.
Tonight I'll light a fire, sing a song.
The sun is low, no doubt
the incredible tonic is ready.

The Beginning of Time

Redemption and mourning:
we have passed the outer gates
and found a highway in the mist.
A wave leaps into darkness.
Step by step, the ocean is a field of light,
the moon a broken compass
in the heart of memory.
I have been here since the beginning of time.
I am my own star reaching back
to shine on the mountains of joy.
I will spend the summer
wearing boots made of sand.
I am a boat, a tree in the mist,
the moon that sails
beyond the clouds and wind.
Leviathan of eternity,
the spindrift eye of everything that is.

The Door of the River

Only one summer world this decade,
red leaves hanging above
the highway, and the door
of the river turned to stone.
When I come here again I will find
that the forest has walked away
and there is only one book
in the library of the future,
and I will forget about the past,
the vanishing trees and mountains.
I'll farm the land around my house:
sugar beets and carrots,
winter wheat and sorghum.
I do not know what else to wish for.
To hear bells ringing in a church,
or a hammer on an anvil.
The past sleeping on a ridge
beyond the lake where coyotes howl.

Thanksgiving Day

Morning, the sun trips a wire
and dances along the river,
clouds part, the wind whispers.
Bells toll in the distance,
swallows drift in the hair of trees.
I am making stars
from granite, flesh from bones.
Bringer of ice to the end of summer.

My neighbor follows the path
beside my house into town.
He'll buy groceries, a lager at the pub,
hear a story he won't remember,
laughter all around.
He doesn't have much to give,
not even sorrow.
Only ice and snow in his bones,
punky firewood, rusted tools.

Stranded on Thanksgiving Day,
I feel spirits watching,
the wind speaking of life
in another land where camels
thread the eyes of needles.
A deer limping across the road.
A lonely dove
cooing from a telephone wire.
I feel as though I could live forever.

What We Knew Before

In the four worlds where the sun sets
I see the dark waterfalls of winter
and the deep roots
of the summer solstice.
I hear a drum beating
beyond the valley of forgetting.
Brother, I will find your address there,
your missing months and years.

I remember your smile when I am sleeping.
I hear your breath in the trees.
Speak to me again of the treasures
I have buried. Tell me I am
no longer a strange ornament.
Together we will wait for the next boat
to arrive—or walk on water
to the farthest shore.

Step by step, the ocean is a field of light,
the moon a compass in the heart
of perfect being. What we knew
before vanishes when the future
steals our memory.
We live as explorers in another
world where stones speak.

Footprints on the Highway

Yesterday and tomorrow
are like stolen alphabets,
calendars of mountains and rivers,
the earth as it rejoices,
footprints on the highway,
two people running beside the ocean,
suddenly beholding love everywhere.
This is how we know who we are:
we study the rainbows and waterfalls.
Friends, family, and loved ones
share stories of oceans
that once formed roads.
When driving downtown,
we notice that all the other planets
are missing. Every moment
is a secret opening to another world.

All the Bridges

I saw a man walking on a bridge.
I saw a man walking on water.
The sun set and all the men
in the water were drowned.

I saw a woman walking across railroad tracks.
I saw a train glide into the sea.
I saw a sunset riding the rails.

I saw a boy flying an airplane.
I saw an airplane in a sky
like a map of ancient cities.
Clouds crinkled like paper,
the sea like a blue tablecloth.

I fell into the sea like a bird without wings,
like a bolt of shining cobwebs,
like a mountain walking on the beach.

Smoke from a burning sun
drifts overhead
and flowers of frost bloom
on all the bridges beyond the sea.

Dream of Departure

I held a picture to the wall
and stepped through it.
I saw volcanoes on the moon,
stars falling from the sun,
a lonely cloud drifting in the sky,
a river overflowing with red fish,
a fire burning in the heart
of the forest. Distant laughter
and echoes of thunder
across a vanishing prairie.

My younger sister remembers
what the rest of us have forgotten:
clouds sing and trees dance.
Wherever I go I will be like smoke
in gathering stillness, a dream
of departure in the wilderness,
the future of lost and found,
the weather that shines like a river
in the valley of stones.

Gathering the Days

My dog ran down to the sea, across
the mountains, the river of sighing,
into the seventh circle of laughter.
We found him by the road
with a smile on his face
and buried him on a hill
overlooking the canyon of tears.
Now I live in a city and follow
accidents from street to street.
I dream every night that nothing
has changed. Lost in silence,
I am gathering the days for burial,
listening for the voice of forgiveness.

What is the tongue? The black sky
of mourning. What are the hands?
Blue stars that have broken free
and fallen like tattoos on the needy.
The sky is a quilt, four-postered,
diamond-patterned, trees and flowers
reflected in the mirror of clouds.
I hear the voices of my ancestors
speaking as the river disappears
and my brothers join a parade
in another city, where spirits
remember what has yet to become.

Beside the Waiting River

I remember the river and the grove of trees,
the snow on the rocks in the garden of ice.
I went there to remember the house in the valley
before I was born, an argument I won
while listening to the voices of the departed,
an ancient civilization breathing in my bones,
trees that bleed, a heart that stammers,
a photograph grown dim like the light of years.
I resisted telling my story because
of the fear elements burning in darkness.
Instead, I rode a blue horse into the forest's breath.
Now I belong to everyone, the king of fear,
the prince of pain. When I fall I don't get up;
I lie in bed like a fossil in the stream
that flows through the veins of another body.
A shadow on the wall, a ghost that lives
like a hangman where a naked light
is shining. At least I still have this boat
that is always drifting in a disappearing culture.

The Holy Hour

On Sunday I sat in church
an hour before the service
and thought about how
there are no hospitals
on the moon and the streets
and back alleys of this village
are like drawings of distant
star systems on the walls
of monasteries. Nothing
has been created or destroyed,
time does not exist. Forget
adding and subtracting,
forget beggars and explorers
who speak the minds of kings.
Travel a different highway
every day, cast a shadow
on the turnpike, make room
for the wind rising in darkness.
Not everyone in this town
knows the pastor's secrets.

III

A Small Tree in a Glass Bowl

The Forest Beyond the Trees

It is April and the stones have not stopping singing.
I place two photographs on the floor,
watch as the flowers of the sun turn to ash.
At first light, the pines are a river too deep to ford,
clouds like seams in the cloth of a new day.
What I saw before is suddenly invisible in a sea of trees.
My neighbor says she will return to dust soon.
Through a window at night, I see her brushing
her long silver hair. Her mourning or betrayal
cannot change what she will soon discover
in her astonishment. What wanders in the forest
is the body of ageless being. After a long sleep,
darkness is like the moon crawling across the plains.
Let the snow gather itself as a door to the universe.

The Light of Faith

Not everything decays beside the road
that leads north to the battlefield
where flames burn like roses
and conversations rise slowly
to the tops of trees,
and the light of faith in the sky
is like a funeral at dusk,
the time of harvest,
the time beyond time, something
we felt but could not explain:
the faces of the lonely, the abandoned.
This is not the country of fear,
so much as indifference.
See how they run
from the world that loves them.

When I Walk Beside the River

A friend has departed from beside
the waterfall where he was sweeping stars
like darkness into a well of shadows.
I will hold his name in my hands,
sing his songs over and over,
live in the house where he was born,
the farm where I was bitten by memory,
the city where I fell, sleepwalking,
from the bridge of my brother's voice.

In his mirrors, truth is reborn,
and in his windows, the past and future
are like the moon without a blueprint.
When I walk beside the river
I hear bells ringing, feel the days passing
like trains bound for somewhere else.
When I find that village
where the anointed live,
I will play a song from the sabbath
like a man with no place to go.

What We See Now

I leave and bring everything back to me.
I say goodbye and then hello.
Let us turn back the clocks
and say farewell to a world
blinking on and off like a dying star.
What we see now
has never been seen before.
The earth lives in the same space as the sun.

My mother's spirit comes to me
at night when the light
of the mountains is turned on.
Joy is moving into the house of sadness.
Green sea of departure,
blue ocean of arrival:
between these is the ship that sails forever.

The Silent Village

The first moon turns from earth
and drifts out into space.
Another moon rises in cold
November air. Years float
like barges past deserted islands,
growing smaller as they pass
the last outpost. Night without
stars, not what we hoped for.

Trees burn in broken bottles,
a fire in the mind of every forest.
In the book of storms, two
seasons soar like jets as the man
on fire leaves his handprint
on a map of my hometown.
He is a wildflower without
baggage or bitterness, a bear
dreaming of his own blackness.

Q and A

What is truth?

> Walls have fallen and stones have become
> the children of what lasts forever.
> Books tear pages from themselves
> and paper the world with ideas.

What is life?

> A black coat flies through the windows
> of heaven and lands in a field of wildflowers.
> Gloves will not speak after a winter
> of blinding snow.

What is chance?

> Time expands in a universe of silence,
> a thought moves with the speed of light,
> bells ring, and truth disappears
> in the waves of a frozen river.

What is rhythm?

> Trees as they bend to the wind of sorrow.
> Soldiers as they doff their helmets
> and drape golden fleece around
> the shoulders of the king of hearts.

What is spirit?

> Black smoke from the river between
> shadow and moon. A house of wood,
> built with hands of steel.

What is time?

> The hat that floats in the river of delusion
> and vanishes in the sea of impermanence.

Pilgrims on Earth

On Sunday after the church service,
things begin to take off:
two blazing sunlit vapor trails,
a rainbow cascading into the valley,
a bird on fire with reflected colors,
a spark in the hallowed stones
along the secret highway to redemption.
Lonely for solace, companionship,
a house on the beach, whatever
attracts the single dweller;
you will be the first to find it,
the first to raise your hand
when the call comes through.
What we see and don't see:
a sacred grove, a gentle breeze
in the offshore realms of our minds.

Goddess of the Sea

I walk beside the ocean
where the goddess of the sea
speaks to me through
the voice of a whale.
I tell her I have been forgiven
and she tells me about
the stars she has sacrificed
in the forest where
blue trees are humming.
Where is this forest, I wonder,
and where are the singing trees?
Look for a rainbow,
the voice of the sea tells me.
In every direction, I see storms
gathering and then dispersing.
Rainbows flying back
and forth through
the windows of heaven.

Words I Will Remember

Each tree in the forest
is a bedroom where
clouds rest their tiny souls.
Years burn in a winter
of secret uprisings—
a tent in that dark country
is on fire. Under the earth
the sun struggles against
an army of shadows.
The voices of birds
echo the language
of the northern wind,
words I will remember
when my house shakes
with the howling of wolves.

Poet of Silence

We still have the poems, a few pictures,
and enough memories to fill a parking lot.
A trip to the borderlands—bless
the guards—a tunnel under a wall,
the door like a tongue:
too many signs to read,
too many languages to memorize.
Welcome your spirit, offer it a place
at the table. Light a fire,
oak and cherry are best.
Bless your body with sage and timothy.
Don't ask about time and how eternity
seems to fill the smallest bottle.
Watch as the horizon moves forward
to greet you. Let dreams
live in the place of forgiveness.
Poet of silence,
I am carrying your burdens for you.
My days are laughing, torn up, plowed under.

Beginning to Listen

We must forget everything
we learned in the forest,
except how stones sing
and fish live beyond time
in a shallow world
of unending darkness.
A bell rings and the people
who live nearby wave their arms
like the far horizons.
Yesterday and today,
images of you and me,
are like a language
we will not understand
when tomorrow arrives.
I am back there now in that
other world where trees speak.

The Cloud of Belonging

All my relatives are gathered
at the base of a mountain,
talking of the days when the sky
touched the earth like a holy hand.
A white buffalo wandered
past the village where an angel
disturbed the river of time,
and the woman who lived forever
married a man who killed
a buffalo in a snowstorm
and used the hide for shelter.
When he came to himself
he was holding a silver rope
from the cloud of belonging,
but he had forgotten the names
of rivers and mountains.
When his memory returned,
he rode his blue horse
between a pair of rainbows.

After the Flood

People are talking in different languages
and birds are flying like words
as they unroll as one scroll
within each sentence.
Every paragraph is like darkness
vanishing as the sun
walks through our garden.
Everything untoward is chipped
from stone. Clouds break
on the beach like silence
on an invisible mountain.
Our dreams are melting in the heat,
our bones lonely
for the everlasting arms.
One by one, the hills reveal an empty river.

A New Narrative

For days now you have searched
for an answer to your prayers.
It is like a feather in the absolute.
Let it go. Let it fall like grace
cascading from the lips
of a new narrative.
You wanted to feel something,
so your village was burned.
Let that go, too. The body
you enter now is not your own.
Time is like a future of perfect circles,
a long marriage in the eyes
of galloping horses, spirits
that flicker like candles
in the squall of traveling moons.
You will return one day and feel
the river between your toes.

Land of Dreams

Almost heaven is born in a canyon
hidden from the sun. My body
is like a stone or a highway
or the joy of looking up at the sky
when clouds have become trees.
Some mornings I am prepared
for adventure in the realm
of whiskey and ash, the land
of dreams around a distant shore.
I hear a bell ringing in a broken tower,
drive a highway that no longer exists.
I open a window in a waterfall
and find a mirror in the forest.

The Voice of the River

After a long journey, refuse to be changed.
Distances do not disturb our view
of background cities. From stars
we hear of life as a shadow
when mountains begin to speak.
I hear a voice from the river.
A woman tells me her son has drowned
and his bones are buried in the forest
where night opens like a door
in a waterfall and birds of prey
are like stones in the dreaming river.
Tomorrow, stars will drop like rain
on the village where the elders
are no longer singing the old songs.
I cannot close my eyes to the darkness.
At night, I remember the voices
calling from the ancient river
where memory is suddenly unleashed.

Moment of Clarity

Where the wind blows there
are fingerprints on sidewalks,
scent of jasmine,
photographs of raindrops,
a small tree in a glass bowl.
Where I am now is one
of those places that reveals
its secrets to everyone.
The moon drifts on the waves
of our thoughts, the river rises,
dams hold. A moment
of clarity is like solitude
at the end of a long journey.
What we don't understand,
the mysteries of being
and becoming,
are greater than we are.

I Want to Remember

Today I am thinking of trees,
mountain pools and waterfalls,
my life at the crossroads of silence,
riding my blue horse between
virgin lakes and the sacred forests
that join hands with the wind.
My horse speaks to me
as if yesterday had never been.
I want to remember how it was:
the fire in the sky and the wings
of the sea. My first love
running on a beach, wearing
her white dress like a cloud.
Soon I will understand the past
and let the future forgive everything.

The Church in the Sky

At night, the earth trembles
and echoes gather in valleys
where waterfalls climb
to the shoulders of mountains.
I see lightning darting
from a blackbird's beak.
Men with shovels have found
the graves of the unjust.
I cannot see them as they dig
beyond the horizon.
My ancestors come when I call.
They lean their shoulders into the wind.
The church in the wilderness
says nothing of our earth.
The church in the sky is a doorway to heaven.

The Singing of the Wind

There is joy in the garden walls,
in the footprints of giants,
where dogs follow the smell of damp hay,
and girls sew their fingers to the dawn.
The singing of the wind
in the hollow stream of stars,
St. John of the Cross drawing
water from the well of stillness.
Grass grows in the shadow of a church.
God is not in the shadow.
We are searching for the white horse,
the wolf in a black uniform.
Not tonight, but tomorrow is rustling
in the meadow where angels
and apostles are beating their drums
in the debris of a new century.

Like a Tombstone

There was something holding me there,
not the snow, not the ice,
not the desert of human emotions.
We lived in the same place,
the same town,
and everything we knew
was like the unknown.
What kept bringing me back
was the cemetery
beside the railroad tracks,
the path beside the creek,
the pond that shouted the names
of my brothers and sisters.
Each rock in the river was like a door
opening in my mind, a flower
blooming in the moonlight.

**Poems in this book previously appeared
or are forthcoming in the following publications:**

Cincinnati Review: "My Brother Running"
Cimarron Review: "The Dogs of Winter"
South Carolina Review: "Beside the Waiting River"
I-70 Review: "Like a Tombstone"
Atlanta Review: "The Forest Beyond the Trees"
SALT: "A Forgotten Language," "Everything I Do
       Involves Forgetting"
Crosswinds: "My Father's House"
Poetry East: "When One Flower Blossoms,"
       "Thanksgiving Day"

About the Author

Michael Malan was born in Missoula, Montana, and educated at Antioch College and Cornell University. He embarked on the Spirit path during a meeting of the Native American Church at Wounded Knee, South Dakota.

He is grateful to the following teachers and friends who have been his mentors and guides over the years: Bruce Fitzwater, Burt Lester, Steve Helmer, Liz Helmer, Joe Eller, Betty Edds, Robin Andersen, and Edith Wells.

In 1999, Malan and Peter Sears founded a small press, Cloudbank Books, in Corvallis, Oregon. Their first book was *Millennial Spring: Eight New Oregon Poets. Cloudbank,* a literary journal (cloudbankbooks.com), was launched in 2009. Malan currently serves as editor.

He is the author of *Overland Park* (Blue Light Press, 2017), a collection of poetry and flash fiction, and *Tarzan's Jungle Plane* (Blue Light Press, 2019), a collection of prose poems. His work has been published in *Epoch, Grist, Washington Square Review, Cincinnati Review, Tampa Review, Denver Quarterly, Poetry East, Hayden's Ferry Review, Potomac Review,* and many other journals.

www.ingramcontent.com/pod-product-compliance
Lightning Source LLC
Chambersburg PA
CBHW032027090426
42741CB00006B/756

9 781421 837031